the art

of

letting go

Poetry for the Seekers

Sanhita Baruah

Dedicated to

all the losses

you and I didn't hold on to

Acknowledgements

I may have written only a handful of prose in a year's time but I have hummed too many poems to myself while I walk, while I travel and sometimes, when I sit down to write.

The first collection of my poems, "The Art of Grieving" was published in the form of an e-book a year back. The immediate response from friends and family made me not give up on publishing my work for the masses.

I deeply thank all my readers for keeping the spark in me alive. Oh! What am I going to do with my life if not write?

My sincere thanks to Rafaa Dalvi for being the one to awaken me last winter to publish my first book of poetry.

My heartfelt thanks to my father, Tilak Prasad Baruah who himself published his work of satirical fiction this year and became a source of inspiration to publish this book.

I am forever indebted to my constant pillars of support and guidance– Bandana Devi (mother) and Rithika Baruah (elder sister).

Special mentions for my sources of motivation– Bhavya Kaushik, Smriti Mahale, Tanmay Jhawar, Rituparna Chakraborty, Sambhav Jain, Suman Surana, Ankur Shrimali, Ankit Naik, Jonali Boishya, Dinesh Madne and Supratim Ghosh.

"Whatever it is you're seeking won't come in the form you're expecting."

HARUKI MURAKAMI

Sanhita Baruah

Hope

Shipwreck

I have kept myself afloat
For so many years, by now...
Ages have passed keeping
My head above water,
My hair above the muck...
I steer the gigantic ship
To every direction it must go,
I look through the lenses so often
Yet I can't find home...

The lighthouse would lead me right,
The beacon would take me home,
I often practice swimming,
And learn to row a boat...

There's this urge to jump ship,
The wait has been too long,
The ship's compass has failed
The path I am on must be wrong...

I would take my final leap
At the sight of the next boat,
At the sight of the next light
I would row the tiny boat
Till the end of the sea,
Till the end of time.

I could swim a thousand seas
I couldn't just stay afloat,
I couldn't sail the ship to shore

So I waited for the tiny boat.
On some faraway island,
I am trained to make a home
I am trained to be a lonely sailor,
I am trained for the creaky boat,
I am trained for dragons in the sea
But not for the comfort of the ship,
I've been prepared for loneliness
But never for love,
I've been prepared for shipwrecks
But never for hope.

Dress Up

It's funny how one's life goes through highs
and lows
But we put on some kohl and brush our brows.
We someday realize we have no one but foes;
So we sit back to paint the nails on our fingers
and toes.

For that might be the way one can drop that
frown,
To let not the world and its people pull you
down,
For I can see my life all blue- the hue I dread
But I can change my hair to a better shade of
red.

I may wake up to find a messy work-life
But I can neatly braid my hair and pretend
it's all fine.

I can find my job dull or whine that it's not
fair
But I can take out a magic wand and curl my
hair.
I may cry all I can, as if I'm trapped in
Medusa's lair
But tomorrow I'll still show up with a
confident flair.

Unread Letters

I hope you still write her letters,
I hope tears still fall from her eyes,
Reading those letters she never found.
And when you look at the letters you never
sent,
I hope it's her eyes that see the love wrapped,
For they no longer need to know the words.
But even when words fail to work magic,
I hope you still believe in your letters...
I hope you still write her letters
But I hope this time,
You sent the letters you wrote...

A Night's Conversation

I turn out the lights
And he turns on the radio,
And it's almost like a routine
The way he approaches the bed
And I approach him.

We smile at each other
With other people
On our minds.

We start with a gentle peck
And then probably a kiss
Of feelings close to disgust.

He kisses my scars
Scars that remind me of wounds-
Wounds that he wasn't a part of.

It isn't love
And we both are in pain,
And we make love,
A good night's sleep is preordained.

I turn out the lights
Inside my head as well.
"Oh, stop thinking."

He turns on the radio
And a million thoughts
Approach his mind.

Tomorrow,
We shall not remember each other
for I have someone else to go to
And he has someone else in his mind.
But we'll smile at each other-
Smile close to disgust.

And we'll call it love
When naked bodies meet
Knowing not,
That love it is not.
For our naked souls await
To be revealed
And a good conversation
Was our sole need.

Beyond

Where does the serpentine road lead?
To the hill's top and beyond.

A tiny hut resides at the end of the road,
The road ends where people do not go.

There rests in peace my muse and love
Within a coffin made of soil and leaves.

Sometimes, she sits atop the mountains
people do not see,
Touching the clouds, she smiles in glee.

And when the wars will end and birds will
sing.
She will turn the serpentine road around,
For a new world to lead.

Shattered

They say when you tell your dreams to the
world
The Universe makes them come true.

I have seen dreams shattered into pieces,
Lying on a bed of thorns, I have seen them go
all wrong.

They say it's dark when dreams become
nightmares,
When dark shadows grow darker,
Forming the shapes of the monsters inside
you.

They say dark is the colour of blood
That oozes out of your eyes when your world
shatters,
Your dreams die, and you break down.

I have seen light creep in the dungeon
Only when there was nothing left behind.

Sunrise

Some mornings the sun won't rise...

You can choose to go back to sleep,
Gulp a glass of water,
Take those pills you need,
Reverse the way your life has been...

Some mornings the sun won't rise

But you can choose to embrace the artificial
lights
Fill your heart up with the sparkling shine
Tiny cracks to be filled with colours,
Twinkling luminance in every corner,
You may wake up and still choose life

Even though some mornings,
the sun won't rise...

Something New

Words engulf him
The way he gulps his scotch
One glass after another.
He grabs his pen
And writes down his love
Pages after pages.
He passes a smile at me
At times when he isn't bothered
About how he looks
When his teeth is shown,
When his hair is uncombed
And she passes him by.
He writes a note for her
Without reading
The stories I've to tell.
He asks me, sometimes,
As he drops his note
In her old letterbox.
His thick eyelashes flutter,
A gulp in his throat,
Drops of sweat
On his forehead,
He fumbles as he utters,
"Have you written anything new?"

Twisted

Of you, I cannot speak
Or so, you think!

Because you thought my bones were a little
easier to break,
My hands and legs a little easier to mend,
Because my ankle is a little more twisted than
what you'd call zero degrees,
Because my limbs are not as strong as yours
could ever be,
You thought I would shut up about the crimes
you did commit,
Because my voice is a little meek
And you have already ignored a thousand
screams.

That day when you broke into my house to
steal,
You realized there was another living
masterpiece,
Quietly hiding behind the couch,
Sobbing and a little scared of the man in front
of her,
"Who'd believe you?" you had shouted
When she threatened to report you
Because only the women with two legs and
two hands
Get broken into by strangers on the streets.

You thought your words would slice into my
mind
Just like the weapons of your hands did to my
skin.
I bleed and so does my skin,
I break and so does the tissue no one was
supposed to touch
Not when I was still a kid.

You leave, triumphed, thinking that was it-
Robbing a house and a child was victory.

But you forget that I have no strong limbs but
I have a strong memory,
My legs were weak but my fingers could
sketch you in a minute,
That my voice is meek but I still speak
And when I speak, a raise a little hell for you.

The cells in the city must have already made
your bed
And although these arms you held so tight
cannot fight
Words, I have heard, are weapons that can
Dear future-prisoner, in the court, we shall
meet again...

You're a Poem

You're a poem,
And one day, I will write you too;
I'll bleed you out
On the blank pages of my past,
I'll read them aloud
Till forever they last.

But you're a poem,
And you'll not last long,
And one day, I'll end you too;
You'll move on
To another poet;
I'll remember you
Like the abandoned lines
Of a forgotten verse.
And may be then we shall meet,
On the other side of those pages,
On the other side of the blue ink,
On the other side of someday.

Starless Nights

Dreary and Tired,
Eyes of the night.
Words too worn out
To yell, to fight.
Drained out of
The hope for tomorrow,
They look at each other,
At each other's sorrow.
Eyes, too used to cry;
They are shut now.
A dark sky,
Another starless night,
3:00 am
And the tale called life.

Take a Risk Today

You do not know you've always been so brave-

For every time you take a breath,
You take the risk of missing another.
Every time you go to sleep,
You take a chance at never waking up.
You take a flight that may fall and crash,
You sit on a car that may burst in flames,
You take the risk of falling
Every time you run,
You take the risk of hitting a pole
Every time you look back,
Even if to see your past.
You take a risk of burning yourself,
Every time you cook on that blue flame.
You take a risk by using that sharp blade...

You do not feel so for it has become so usual-
If only you could remember
the first day you took a flight, sat on a bike,
fell on the ground, burnt your hand,
or cut your finger...

And if you take such hundred risks every
single day,
If you trust yourself enough now
to not fail in those habitual ways,
How can you not show courage
And take your first step
Towards that big risk today?

Ripples

If the ripples in the bed of tears
Had to mean something to me
It would be the way they vanish
After minutes of creating chaos.
They leave no scars
As if no stone was thrown,
As if no human had touched,
As if the chaos meant nothing
But just a noisy welcome
For the guest called peace.

If the ripples had to mean something
They would mean the world
Could still heal,
Could still make way
For more humans, more stones
Could still hold the tears
And make home for more..

Closure

Closure 101

It isn't fences with barbed wires
And a note saying you're not
Allowed to walk on the grass.

It is an open door-
You may choose to enter,
You may choose to leave.
Do as you please...

After Years

So many years have gone by
And age has made both of us
A lot older than we used to be,
A little wiser than we used to be.
And when the yesteryears
Enter stealthily through the doors
Of a veiled moon and a dark cirrus,
We look back at what we used to be
And what we have become today.

So many years have gone by
And I don't see a single sign of you
And you see me not in who I am today.
I have changed as I should have -
I have built a small hut in a new village now.
You still are in the city we used to live in.
And maybe we'd have been so much happier
now,

But I have changed as I should have
And you, you still have those grey hairs
Like the rays of moonlight falling on my face
now.
And when I have changed as I should have,
You still live in the city we used to live in,
Looking the way you used to look,
And maybe, just maybe, you haven't changed
a bit,
The way you should have changed.

Unique

The same tree has different shades of green;

Each leaf is unique, growing on the same twig.

Some veins wiggle too much,

Some networks- almost a mush.

Blossoming buds of the same branch

Do not take the same time to grow.

Then how do you think you'd fit in

In this strange world,

Away from home ?

Instead

My child of grief!

Hurt you must have been,

Inevitable, crying may seem,

But dear, whenever you're sad,

Just look at yourself,

And ask if it's necessary,

Weep, if you must,

If you really really must,

But do not forget

To ask yourself,

"Why not write a poem, instead?"

Habits

I let you go like some old habits of mine-
Checking your Facebook profile every minute
I touch my phone,
Reading our old messages for signs that would
tell you don't love me anymore,
Putting a burning cigarette in my mouth
every time I thought of you,
Exhaling the smoke every time I realized you
aren't with me.

But such are the habits that do not die-
You come back to me one more time,
You collide with me on a busy street on some
Saturday morning, looking at someone else's
photos from that phone in your hand;
I let you go like the wine of Venice I swear I
would never drink again,
I let you go like the promise of never writing a
poem again
Yet I hold a new bottle of wine dearly in
Vienna,
A few blank pages and a new pen sit by my
side in the cold nights when I would sit in a
train and try hard not to think of you.

But such are the ways with thoughts-
When I close the doors, they find a new
window to come in,
Rotten like the smell of the dried fish you used
to cook,

Fresh like the love bites on your neck that I
don't recognize,
Disturbing like the memories I have dug
graves for some five years ago,
Like the way I don't forget my own mother
tongue even if I hadn't spoken in that
language for years.

But such are the ways with the way we talk-
That your dark grey eyes wouldn't look at me
anymore,
That you'd speak but only to say something in
a language belonging to people who once ruled
us using words that don't resonate with your
feelings,
That you would look back but only to check if
you forgot something,
That you would see my tears but think it is
the lack of sleep in my eyes,
That you would see my smile but not smile
back at me anymore,
That you would not understand why I do
things I do the way you used to read my mind
only a few years ago,
That you would see my burning cigarette but
think it is just a new habit I picked.

But such are the ways of my habits-
That every hour is a closure, every hour I quit
Only for a new beginning but the same old
sh*t.

Masks

I hope it's you
The face you show me every morning,
For I have torn masks before,
I have detached pretty pink masks from dark
red faces,
I have burned those wooden masks so that
they can
Reflect the faces they hide.

They don't.

They veil a different anatomy altogether,
A face that only a mother could truly love,
A face that would push me to trauma for a few
months,
A face that brings along depression and
loneliness.
I have fancied those faces would one day turn
white,
Or a lighter shade of grey or blue.

They don't.

They bathe with blood every night I kiss them
goodnight.
They have bathed in the blood they stole from
someone else alike.
Every time I pull out such masks
Stuck to their skin
Knowing not the thin boundaries
For they have, over the time, erased,

A part of me dies forever.
I fancy that they would return someday
Digging graves for their fancy masks.

They don't.

Every morning I wait
While I see prettier masks, colored yellow and
peach,
Hiding the red, the dark grey and the green.
I hope it's you
As I touch your face,
My fingers searching for boundaries made.
I fail to find the thin lines on your face,
I hope they are wrinkles of the man I date.
You steal a kiss and I check if it's blood on
your lips,

I can't find signs of your mask, so I wear one
instead.

Seashells

Someday I will pick up shells
of every colour
And probably even rob the sea
of its wonder

Yet I won't find a single piece
That'd resemble
the broken pieces
I gathered years ago
Thinking
Those grains of sand were whole...

Loss

Remnants of a smile on a stone-cold face
And maybe you can fool everyone again

That death isn't as painful as we make it to
be...

Some tears bottled up from months gone by-
You'd say judge not how one deals with loss...

Dying dreams like drops of dew under a rising
sun,
You'd laugh; they don't chain your ankles
anymore...

We'd cry for we wouldn't know any better
And make stories of your new whereabouts,
Playing MJ songs and laughing at your own
jokes...
Or in a make-believe world of hope,
Somewhere in peace in a dreamless sleep...

Faces

A second of eternity
Pouring into a frail heart,
Mouthful of love
And handful of trust.
Wounds that lasted
But only for a moment,
Have turned to rotten flesh,
And used-to-be-lips-and-a-face.
Then love comes again
Like a rainbow on a clear-sky-day.
The dark clouds must have
Withered away in pain.
A new skin appears now,
Fresh and unsullied
To be wounded again
But this time, with memories.

Moonlit

Blind eyes of the night,
Half a moon to gaze at,
Half a moon to cry for.

She steps on broken hearts,
Pieces of fierce glass
That used to be mirrors.

She walks a little too close
To the burning walls of hell.
The gates will burn too;
The fire can no longer contain
The wave of iced hearts.

She picks the broken pieces
Till her fingers bleed,
Till those walls turn to ashes.
She steps on the ashes,
Till they embrace the ground
Till one can no longer tell
Ashes from the soil.A slow death, she says,
Is the cure to all pain.
And her last world is
Now ash, soil and blood.

She flies to a new world,
Of iced hearts and blind eyes.
Half a moon to gaze at,
Half a moon gazing back.

Farewell

When you see time passing you by
And you know you can't hold it back,
May be you can plead and beg
But you know she just won't wait,
When you see your brilliant tomorrow
Becoming a feeble and weak past
And you know he isn't as great now
As you thought he would be someday,
When you see the world
Bidding you a veiled good-bye,
When you see those who stay
Aren't even willing to try,
When you realize they just hurt
And pull you back by a strong thread,
When you know you want to go
But the thread just becomes a rope
And pulls you back even more,
You know you must leave, boy!
You must leave when you still can,
And when time flies but extends her hand to
you
You must know you should leave, boy!
For when you look back to smile
You see thorns, pits and rotten faces
And then you must know what to do-
To smile anyway and bid a gentle adieu...

Love Unrequited

For love that went wrong,
I write tonight this song
Of stoics and emotions,
Of hatred and devotions.

For the man who never kept his words,
For the woman who conceived each to be true,
For the broken promises and hopes high,
For the lost love and solace found,
For the letters unwritten and songs sung,
For the million tears and smiles few...

For the woman who wanted to fly,
For the man with wings broken,
For the dreams shattered and heights
unreached,
For the million places yet unseen,
For the vows forced and rules breached...

For the man who loved with a frail heart,
For the woman too strong to falter,
For the anxieties felt and her insouciance,
For the feelings untold and truths confessed,
For the first song and their last dance,
For the realities that hurt,
And imaginations that solaced...

For the woman whose courage was all she
had,
For the man who shattered her only asset,

For the fears instilled by the cruel laughs,
For the claims of love and scars of war,
For the battles fought and lost,
For the courage feigned,
For the innocence that left,
For the life regained...

Nightmares of the Past

From ages, beaten, rotten,
He rises from his own ashes.
He touches the skin, venomous,
Of the one who had breathed the fire.

He burns bright, with envy,
With all the hatred within.
The skin bleeds and wails
On the mummified corpse
Of its own sins-
Its past deeds.

The past rises high
And swallows the dead eyes first.
The skin, once venomous,
Lies at the mercy of its own reflection.

Justice, they say,
Takes a long time to act...
But, they can only heave a sigh
When they finally see
The Time isn't as far
As it seemed to be...

Together

You too will separate-
Despite the identical shadows you make,
Being the exact image you see in the mirror,
Carrying the rhythm of tiny heartbeats
Like equinoxes staying forever.

But some day, some months later-
I will find you back
Like the pair of earrings I lost last year,
Found again at a friend's backyard,
Never to lose one and keep the other
Until the time I dropped one again
On a busy road, on a Friday night,
Almost losing hope
About keeping the bond they hold,
Till the time a stranger came
To hand me the piece I lost
And ask me if it's real gold.

Oh, it is real.
I answer.

Some Mornings

Somedays I wake up early
to see the sun rise nonchalantly
as if last night didn't happen.
It peeps through my window
before it steps up
to face the world.
I sometimes muster enough strength
to uncover myself
with the drenched sheets of last night
and get on my feet
to see it looking at me
probably, lovingly.
But every morning,
it goes away before I can see it.
Every morning it steps away
along with its warmth,
and I
can only see it leaving... .

Chasing Eternity

How nonchalantly we made promises of a love
eternal
And in the quest for eternity
We forgot how to not forget each other,
I had forgotten how it felt like
To be in his presence,
How he would talk of the faraway stars
As we sit under the moonlit sky...
I had forgotten his perfume
And he had forgotten
How my cheeks turn red
Every time I caught a glance of him.

In the quest for eternity
I wrote a million poems,
Letters I would not share...

We had forgotten how it felt like
To live in the "reality" people created.
We left things unsaid
Like we see in the movies written on ideas
created by Shakespeare...
I would cut my wrists,
Drink wine to remember
And recite Bukowski and Plath
In the quest for the eternity they derived...

But most of the pages life did unfold,
Were nothing like the books he read,
Or the poems I wrote...

Life moved on,
One memory after another...
We kept forgetting
Each moment we thought we'd cherish.

Yesterday, I saw him again
His picture on my "news feed"...

I had forgotten how to love him,
So I drop him a "like".
He had forgotten how we would talk for hours
To forget about reality,
So he dropped me a "Hi".

From late night talks to Facebook chats,
From long letters to simple "sup?"s
We reduce, we shrink,
The magic of the stars,
We forget the love
And remember our quest for eternity
Turn into a busy day and tiring night..

Run...

Someday you'll meet someone
Who's gonna look at you in awe-
Flying high, wings all spread...

And wonder how it would be like
To clip those wings,
Tie those feet down
And cage you forever...

When you hit the ground,
Remember to run...

Burning Bridges

I set them on fire,
The pillars of withered leaves
Like promises long broken.
The bridge collapses
On a sea of grief.
I set them on fire
Like there was no yesterday
Looking at this morning
With remorse and a hidden pain.
Ages have elapsed
Like a strand of hair
That loses its identity over time,
Turning pallid painlessly.
I set them on fire-
The long tresses you so loved once,
Touching my neck,
And down my spine,
Once or twice, a gentle peck.
I have burnt bridges,
More times than I have lit a cigar
Or held you in my arms.
Today I pin them down,
I collect the ashes-
Another bridge to build
With grey pillars of
Infidelity and torture.
Love, they call it
While I prepare for it to kindle.

Not Being Enough

A world full of "certainties"
All the plans, all the vanities.
Where black covers the white
Suited in "confidence"- the constant fight.
A million roads I dream to take
One destination, knowing not I turn where.
A green veil covers for two years, some two
decades.
But the "plan" awaits, new roads to make.
I pant, I struggle, I do my best
While they say,

"You are, dear, but so inadequate".

Binary Life

My car moved when I typed 1
It stopped at each 0
I type 1 and the lights were on,
At every 0, it was dark again...

I look away from the perfect screen
Through a glass window covered with dirt,
And I see beyond the translucence
A dimly lit house on the hillside,
A broken door left ajar,
A worn out roof that'd still let
A few raindrops seep in,
A man limping his way home
the way he would have run if he could.
I see the imperfections
Of the enormous tree
Under which a child could still be drenched-
One drop at a time.

I see a half-torn ten dollar bill,
Lying near some worm-ridden mangoes
The owner of the tree couldn't pluck on time,
Useless as both could be, the way
A writer would think away his time,
Without words to put on the paper.

I come home late at night
Another day of programming LEDS
and wheels of the tiny robot car,
Coding 1 or 0, I kill my day,

44

Only to find my night dimly lit
Like the house on the hillside,
Not dark enough,
Not bright enough.
I paint the walls of my room white,
The furniture in it- all black
Only to find my life a little grey-
Impossible to love,
Improbable to hate...

Moving On

Writers don't move on.
They make love with solitude,
They take sorrow in their arms.
They run their fingers down grief's spine.
They touch words gently
And force themselves on a river of tears.
They let masochism win;
so when they bleed,
It's Utopia for them.

Writers don't move on.
They stumble on memories.
They recall something that was eons ago.
They embrace regrets
And make love with retrospection.
And when they do,
They make memories their concubine,
And then they sleep on past's lap,
Because they're writers
And writers don't move on...

The Writer

Of years of solitude

And a final downpour,

Of dreams broken

And all the pieces ashore,

I wondered where went that river

Of all the possibilities.

The pen was lying dead

On a blank paper;

The ink overflown

Drenched my soul;

I wondered if I could ever make right

The massacre I left behind.

I wondered if I could

Ever do what's right.

They told me I was a writer

And that made my life.

Illusions

I think of the words I would like to say

Of love, of separation and your brief stay.

I think of you as I walk the town

On lonely evenings on the nearby lawn.

You quietly follow me on a gentle morning,

I turn around and you're no longer near.

I write the words on a piece of paper.

I write a poem; I write you a letter.

You touch my hand and I cease to write,

I turn around and I see you fade away.

I think you're gone and I need to move on.

I swallow the words, I bury it all.

I tear the paper; I let you go

While you stand there, mutely watching it all.

Tomorrow

Yesterday, life was a bed of roses;
I introduced a few thorns
And they left me bleeding.
I held them close
Till it hurt no more.
I let go of them
So I bleed no more.
I smiled and I hoped
For scented haze.
There was no pain,
But no beauty stayed.
The petals were gone
And away were the leaves.
And when Tomorrow looked back,
He laughed and said,
"Oh, life's no fun,
Without a single thorn."
He was out of my reach,
So, I clung to Today
Till Today came to me
And whispered, "You fool,
I never leave,
I always stay,
Like the thorn in your heart,
Your glee and your sorrow.
Now forget the roses of Yesterday.
And go, chase Tomorrow."

Set You Free

I saw the shackles

That made you bleed.

I wiped your tears;

I, too, wept.

I saw the shackles

That bound you so;

I saw them cut into your flesh.

I didn't see-

They were, but, me.

My tears and my hopes,

Expectations and more so.

When I did remove

My blindfold,

I set you free,

I let you go.

Your Name

I wrote your name in a million letters,

On the pillars of love,

On the walls of heart,

But as each day passes by,

I love you a little less,

And that might be the thing about love,

That today you remember my name

and I forgot yours...

Love

I'm far from being a romantic person. Loving? Not at all. I giggle at the wrong time. My laugh is too loud. I dance weirdly. I often find myself away from people or I find a way to push them away.

But I giggle, laugh and dance anyway.
And whenever I find myself alone, I sing, I think and I write. That's the closest to love that I can ever be. And when I hug the trees and kiss the sunset, when I admire the birds fly and I dance on the beach, that's the closest to romance that I can ever be. I make poems in my head. I make them all the time.

I have always been in love. I'm still in love. I pour all my love to the notepad I write on. I romance the pen. The poems that are still lingering in my head, they say I'm incurably romantic. I still keep my poems. I live more in my imaginations than in reality. And if that's not love, I don't know what else is.
I don't need a him or a her. I'm in love with love itself. I'm a story in another story. I'm somewhere beyond romance. I'm somewhere near love. In between all the love in the air and the romance in the souls, I'm eternal - I'm a poem...

A Traveler's Saga

What are these days I have found myself in!
The backpacks I carry no longer feel that
heavy;

What have they lost if not for a few coins, a
few notes,
some letters written long ago, a few locks, a
few clothes?
Or is it the loss of some fears, some shackles,
some thoughts tied to my waist belt several
years ago?
Where is the fatigue? Where are the tears that
used to drench my pillow?
Where has gone the inability to wake up in
the morning and the desire to sleep that
followed?

Today, every time I close my eyes, my dreams
wake me up and I need to write.
Where is the indolence, the procrastination,
the perceived lack of the "limited time"?

What is this insouciance called?
Where have eloped the incessant need for love,
money and the things I've already sold?
Why Plath has shut her eyes today whom I so
deeply adored?
Bukowski's Bluebird is set free now while
Sahir's pleas I dearly hold,

Because when he asks his muse not to leave
before the fall of the dusk
My muse cures my day, lures my night and
finds some more of my trust..

what do I call this courage that I rely less on
the metaphors today?
I am more than heard, more than understood,
more than being just okay.

What do I call this love for the stars unseen,
the familiar aroma in the air
the sound of the leaves fluttering as the wind
gushes by my hair?

In my backpack, some great memories I have
kept
A stranger's smile, a traveler's note she left on
my bed,
A black burnt pebble from dirty mountains in
Greece,
I have picked up with fervour, even a pine
cone to be packed.

But how do I keep away the only fear I see
now?
That someday, when I am back on earth, back
on the ground
Away from these half-built walls, these lit up
streets, these lost clouds,
Maybe I won't ever be the same, the way I am
here today, the way I am now.

Permanence

I hung awkwardly from the branches of the
tree of permanence
I couldn't fall to the ground,
I couldn't sweep the air,
Fly from leaf to leaf...

The soil would touch my bare body,
My soul would cling to another tree...

I hung awkwardly by the edge of my fingers...

In the world of all or none,
Of rain or the sun,
I hang in the sky like a dark grey cloud,
In-between,
Just for fun!

You and I

Somewhere far,
In another constellation of stars,
Maybe you're right
And maybe I'm wrong,
And maybe I'm not as sick and frail and
unsound,
And maybe you stay
Like the darkest of nights that didn't leave
today.
A thousand years would go by,
Only to let in a thousand more.
Maybe we smile
There
Lying beneath the countless clouds of a
faraway sky.
Maybe time stands still
For it no longer matters
Or maybe it gently passes by
Like the breeze from a land we visited once.
Once, Twice or thrice, maybe we shed tears
too
On the wounds of distant scars
Slowly healing
The way rainbows disappear.
Maybe we smear dirt
On each other's faces
Like children play
With their eyes closed
But hearts open,
And maybe we no longer deny

That there still exists true love
Somewhere far
Beneath the same sky we look at tonight,
Love that overpowers eternity,
Oblivion and destiny.
Love, when it is just you and me.

Detours

Huge trucks coming from the other side
And small cars waiting to overtake you
You might want to give them way
For they seem to be in such a rush
But darling, if you take a left
You may crash on the brick-wall
You may wish to go a little right
But there's a head-on waiting for you there
Slow down, no need to step on it
For sometimes you don't take a detour
You may reach your destiny a little later
You wouldn't know for the road is not clear
But you are going ahead,
As long as you don't stop,
Don't take turns,
Give some way but not the entire path,
So dear,
You
Just
Slow
Down...

Forgotten Forevers

If only truths were spoken,
I can say forevers can be counted,
On the tiny fingers of love
Born a few years ago,
On the walls painted red,
Every year on the same date.

But love has grown up now.
The red walls have been repainted,
This time, on another date,
Only to be repeated year after year,
One false forever after another.

And truths, these days, are spoken
The same way promises are made,
With gritted teeth and crossed fingers.

At the end of the day,
All smiles seem fake,
The fake forevers remain
To be counted upon the stars,
One after the other,
Some forgotten,
Some too dim to be seen,
But a forever, nevertheless,
Another star to keep.

Magic

I wasn't old enough
When I first believed in magic.
Over the years, I have learned
To believe in it,
Even more.
Believe that doors will open,
Or at least, a window will do;
Believe the bars will be shattered,
Or at least, they will melt
The way blocks of ice-cream do.
I wasn't old enough,
When I first saw magic,
In a stranger's smile,
In a bar of chocolate
Handed to me out of the blue.
Over the years, I have seen
Magic still lingering around me.
I have believed in magic,
I still do.
The way I stumble and fall,
The day when things can't go more wrong,
The way it's all good again,
Faint smiles
And the tears I wipe.
And I still see magic
Before I go to sleep
The way the bird near my window
Probably smiles with its weird beak.
And everyday I wake up,
The bird awaits my call,

It flies away
As I take my morning stroll.
Gestures of kindness
And the humble people I meet,
I believe there is magic,
At every step, in every deed.
I am old enough now,
And I still believe in magic.
So when I smile at you,
I hope you do too.

Someday

Someday we will sit again
Where we so lovingly used to do.
We will talk of all that's been
And all that we missed too.

We'll look into each other's eyes,
We'll get back all that we need.
We'll sit and smile and see
Love, eventually succeed.

The wonderful evening
Will bring a beautiful night.
Love, we will cherish
When we reunite.

And so someday I'll laugh off
All the years I stayed maroon.
But all I can hope for now
Is that someday comes soon.

The River

Under the sweltering Sun,
I lost few drops of mine,
Vapourizing into the hot air
Oh, I burned, I cried...
I writhed with the bend
Built by some men
I coursed the way it sent me,
Along the way, I went.
I collided with a mighty rock
I sighed, I needed to rest,
It changed my course, my way
A new way, I went.
Some thirsty birds,
Some time with me, they spent
I beamed at them,
While they drank some of me
And then they left.
I have been sad, at times,
Lonely and blue;
At other times, I would just be free
And blue would be my hue.
I went a long way;
I knew not my destiny.
Often, it would just be me
on a long journey.
I was chained by each bend,
I was forced to move by each hit,
It was my little inferno
And I, it's bound self.
Alas, the time came

For me to be free,
When I lost my true self
To adjoin the sea.

After Note:

And maybe life isn't as hard as it seems to be
Every day could be a mess, but darling, you see
One of the few places you will always find peace
Owes its breeze to the constant chaos in the sea ...

Falling

A couple of hours more
and those dreams will,
once again, burn bright

only to turn into ashes
the moment you look the other way...

There has to be a restlessness
and a certain feeling
that says you're going to fall..
AGAIN

Yet you hope, against all odds...

you jump, and you pray
and believe when you say
what if this time you don't fall
what if this time you fly

Dance in the Storm

She swirls around the same old swing,
Like leaves that float and fly for a new breeze,
The same park where benches lay adorned,
The same garden of memories, of love and
lovelorn...
A gentle drizzle that comes every eve,
Does make her not smile nor blink.
She awaits the rain like a writer embraces
metaphors,
A drizzle isn't for the child who dances in the
storm.
Of rain that washes away the petrichor it
brings,
A downpour of a hail of bullets, and she calls
it spring.

Not a Poem

He says 'tis not poetry what you write.
Where are the stories, where are the rhymes?
Though we look into each other's eyes for
hours
From one sunset to another sunrise.
He says 'tis not love if we await another day.
Where are the words you and I didn't say?
He says 'tis not about my daydreams.
He says we don't hold hands very often.
For the world is filled with contemporary
poets,
He says mine don't fit this world of substance.
Where does the heart of your poem lie?, he
asks.
A poem's not a breeze, long, that doesn't last.
A minute longer that doesn't stay,
'Tis not a poem, 'tis what your feelings say.

A floating second on someone's news feed,
No dearth of meanings for those who read,
Not my stories but 'tis what I think,
I say I don't write poems, I just write dreams.

No More

I promised him, I won't write a poem again...
It's been more than a month now
Yet I have written a million on my heart
A million on my mind, my soul, in between
conversation, in pieces, in whole...
I have written them time and again, never to
be read,
never to be heard, never to be told
For I kept a promise I dearly hold,
Never to write a poem again, unless I am told
Oh, the pictures can't describe what I feel,
Where are the metaphors? I am done with the
reel.
Where are the words? For you can't read my
mind.
Where are the innuendos or the shy gestures
from the divine?
Oh, how can I be myself if I don't pause to
think, to write.
To experience is heaven, but no more poems is
a sacrilegious crime
I break the promise today, to unveil another
one
No more poems on paper, but many more on
the leaves of my mind...

My First Swimming Lesson

I found it strange
how men swam in the pool
without seeming to feel
even a tad bit uneasy
about their less than perfect bodies,
hairy,
dark,
with proud paunches
wearing a swimsuit
that was nothing more than a boxer
While I,
Another imperfect woman,
Shivered in my suit,
Wondering if more than my contours were
visible,
Even though it was dark,
Even though the swimsuit covered
what's "necessary to cover".

My first swimming lesson
And instead of feeling proud
for having dared,
for having tried,
A million thoughts
Crossed my fearful mind.

The fat belly.
The fat arms.
Hairy armpits.
Sunburns.

Chlorine.
Shape.
Shame.

Thighs too flabby.
Hips too large.
Hold your breath.
Keep your head down.
Pull the suit's edges
Let it cover some more skin.
I need to wax.
I need to look thin,

My first swimming lesson
And before feeling
the fear of water
I felt shame.

And if perfection is the need
only for women.
Oh, I tell you, it's a disease
that brings nothing but shame.

So, as my feet touched the water beneath,
To kill the shame, to feel free
I realized what I really, really need.
I needed not to burn calories,
Nor a little waxing.
All I really needed
Was to not think.

After Death

You're all words,
When it is your death.
For people by then
Would have forgotten
How to love you, again.
They would remember
You not, for your deeds
Were forgotten too soon.
You lived on the smell
Of ephemeral cigarettes,
On the taste of bitter beer
And the whiskey that burns
Your guts as it vanishes.

What is it that you'll leave behind?

Your beauty was forgotten
When you succumbed
To the wrinkles of aging.
Your smile is no longer charming
When you hide the gum
That misses a tooth.

So what is that you'll leave behind?

Probably, those words,
Never spoken,
Only written down,
On the bark of a tree
To be read by strangers
Who know nothing about your struggle.
And when the tree dies,
And the soil embraces your words,
Probably it is then
That your soul will rest
As your words will finally leave love
For the soil,
That you couldn't.

Yours Truly

Like the vastness of an ocean;
As strong as a woman can be,
As weak as the sign of first love;
Like two lovers meet for the first time,
Like death separating a couple, divine;
As difficult as life can turn out to be,
Like the mystery the Universe's end holds;
Like the little girl who wants a balloon,
Like Cindrella's prince in the ballroom;
Like a mother giving birth to her first child,
Like a baby holding your fingers tight;
As leaves change yet the root does not,
Like the same old house on the same old plot;
Like happiness, yet,like a profound sigh,
My love thrives as I say I'm thine.

Grow

Do not let the world tell you not to bloom
Just because they aren't ready for you
Just because few days after they bloomed
They died on a barren land, in the rain

You may face the same fate
But deep down you would know
It's better to die blooming
Than choosing to never grow...

Home

Some days I wake up and decide to be
somewhere else,
I hit the road just to keep myself sane,

In a world of healthy breakfasts and scanty
dinner
I lay my back on a wooden armchair,
Fill my stomach with some badly made tea,
A couple of cookies and serenity... In a world
of feeding pigeons off one's hand,
Some ants feed off my feet
Half-immersed in the dusty sand,
I give way to tiny crabs in a hurry
While see nature wiping my footprints.

I shut my eyes and silently call out to the sea
Sometimes I hear her say, "Come home with
me"

Sunshine in my Backyard

From the last two days I've seen no night,
No darkness, no dusk, no rains, no blight.
My orchard's flowers seem to shine bright.
Birds chirp around and butterflies alight.
Grandmother's woven the sweater, at last,
of Brother's embroidered shirt's size.
From the last two days I can hardly count
The days of happiness I've lived in disguise.
Summer ain't so hot nor have I seen Winter's
chill.
From the last two days, life doesn't seem so
hard.
No, don't bring me the stars from the sky,
I'm planting sunshine in my backyard.

∞ ∞ ∞

"*You have to keep breaking your heart until it opens.*"

RUMI

Sanhita Baruah, born and brought up in Guwahati, Assam, has been writing poems since the age of ten. She has been embracing poetry ever since and had started her blog 'Pens and Pages' in 2011. With an MBA in Marketing from MDI Gurgaon, she is a business development professional by the day and a poet by the night. Her short stories and articles aim to connect to the masses and have been published in various anthologies and magazines. She is driven by the purpose of making a difference in people's lives and she believes in beginning with small steps.

The Art of Letting Go, 2018

Printed in Great Britain
by Amazon

42447887R00057